How to Care for Your Snake

CONTENTS

We would like to thank the following for permission to photograph their stock:
Hansards Pet Centre, Romsey

Photos by:
Colin Jeal, David Alderton, David Green, Linda Lewis

KINGDOM

©2001 by Kingdom Books PO9 5TT ENGLAND

INTRODUCTION

Welcome to the world of snake-keeping! You are reading this book, so you are interested in snakes. If you are interested in snakes, it means you are not influenced by the bad publicity snakes tend to get. It is true that people have an instinctive fear of snakes, but society reinforces that fear. Also we are told that snakes are filthy (they are very clean), slimy (not so), dangerous (only relatively few are venomous), and generally repulsive.

The truth is that snakes are beautiful animals. They are as interesting and colourful as birds, fish and any other creature that people like to look at and admire. Apart from that, many snakes make excellent pets!

As a newcomer to the world of snakes, I hope that you will enjoy this book. It is designed especially for the beginner - a person who has never kept a snake before. It looks at the basics of selecting a snake, how to feed and house it in order to keep it healthy, and discusses a selection of the best snake species to start with, based on those which are easy to keep and which you are likely to be able to afford.

A Western ribbon snake, *Thamnophis proximus proximus.*

As with any pet, snakes have advantages and disadvantages. First we'll look at the advantages. Snakes are easy to care for. They do require some daily attention, but do not demand the emotional attachment you have to give a dog or cat. Snakes are quiet - your neighbours will never complain about the noise! Snakes are very clean and are not particularly smelly. They do not eat much in comparison with other pets and most are perfectly happy with only one or two feedings a week. Snakes are often long-lived, and many match or exceed the lifespan of a dog or cat.

But there is a down side, although the disadvantages are not really the snake's fault. The main one is that many people are afraid of snakes, and the mere sight of one sends some people into hysterics.

This leads me to a very important point. The responsible snake owner is not someone who keeps a snake because it is 'cool' or 'trendy'. Too often I've seen people use snakes for shock value - carrying them around on the street, thrusting them in other people's faces and generally being childish. Some people seem to get pleasure out of seeing a snake kill live prey; apart from this being unpleasant, these people may actually be harming their pet.

A snake owner should be genuinely interested in the biology of the animals and not use them as cheap playthings and status symbols.

SELECTION

What kind of snake is best for you? First, how much money do you have to spend - probably you don't want to spend too much on your first snake. How much space is available in your home for the snake's cage? Will the snake grow? Make sure that you can house it comfortably when it is an adult. There is a big difference between a 60cm (2ft) garter snake and a 3.5m (12ft) boa constrictor. Later, I discuss particular snake species which will help you make a more informed choice but, for now, I will just say this: don't take on more snake than you can handle.

It is best to get your first snake from a specialist pet shop or breeder who stocks captive-bred snakes which are cleaner (fewer parasites), feed better and are tamer than wild-caught specimens.

By watching a snake in its pet shop cage, how do you know if it is healthy? First, it should be alert, watching all movement in and near its cage with bright, clear eyes. Beware of sluggish, unresponsive specimens.

Examine the snake's skin carefully, especially the spaces under the scales where ticks and mites often hide. Snake ticks are big, looking like bumps sticking out from beneath the scales. Mites are tiny creatures, black or dark red, and can be seen moving around. Avoid any snake with these external parasites.

Look at the snout and mouth. Red marks, sore swollen patches or mucus in or around the mouth area indicate mouth rot. Avoid any snake you suspect might be affected.

It can be hard to tell if a snake has been feeding well. Ask the shop proprietor if the snake is eating, and find out what it has been eating and when it was last fed. A captive-bred snake should come with a feeding record. Be cautious if you can see a pronounced ridge running down the middle of the snake's back. A starving snake begins to cannibalise its own muscle tissue, and the loss of dorsal muscles causes the tops of the vertebrae to protrude, appearing as a ridge. Such a snake is, almost literally, skin and bones - don't buy it.

As a beginner it is hard to know if your new snake will be healthy but it will help if you follow the above guidelines. If possible, always choose a captive-bred animal which should be free from parasites, feed well and have a good temperament. You should end up with a healthy animal which will give you years of enjoyment and open up the fascinating world of reptiles.

Right: This Sinaloan milk snake is obviously used to being handled. However, milk snakes can be fussy eaters, so are not recommended for beginners.

HANDLING

One of the most important things when handling a snake is to assess whether or not it is tame before you attempt to pick it up. For safe handling you need the following equipment: a snake stick (like a small shepherd's crook), thick leather gloves, and a snake sack to put the snake in. If your snake is not tame it will do one of two things: strike at you because it thinks you are a threat or strike at you because it thinks you are food.

A snake that regards you as a threat will strike repeatedly, often hissing with its mouth open. It will not bite and hold or coil around you. The best way to deal with this snake is to be patient and make sure you do not appear as a threat. Use the snake stick to hold it down gently just behind the head and then get your other hand around its body to pick it up. Most snakes calm down once they are picked up but, if yours continues to strike, be careful not to drop it. Gradually, the snake will stop seeing you as a threat and, although it may never enjoy handling sessions, it will stop striking at you. Please note that some species of snake will never tame and these should not be kept unless you are experienced with snakes.

You have a potentially dangerous situation when a snake thinks you are food, especially if you are dealing with a 4.5m (15ft) python!

A snake that thinks you are food will grab hold and coil around your arm. Unravel it gently, starting from the tail. Once the snake is straight, quickly and gently submerse the head underwater until the snake lets go but be very careful not to drown it. It should take no more than two or three seconds for this to work.

To prevent this happening in the first place, make sure that you have not been handling anything that might make you smell like food - such as rats or mice - as even the tamest snake will strike if it thinks you are dinner. Touching the snake very gently on the head with a snake stick or whilst wearing gloves will prevent it from confusing you with food.

If you are worried about being bitten, or you are dealing with very large, unknown snakes, it is advisable to wear gloves. Never grasp a snake tightly or try to restrain it. Guide it where you want it to go. Also avoid holding it behind the head. Never handle your snake just after you have fed it as you may damage the internal organs. Instead, allow it to rest at least a day before picking it up.

An Everglades rat snake being held gently by its handler.

HOUSING

It is not difficult to house a snake. The easiest cage to obtain is an all-glass aquarium, available from any pet shop. The tank should be at least as long as the snake and as wide and high as half the snake's length. If you are buying a young snake, allow some extra room so that it does not become cramped as it grows.

Place the cage well away from windows or other draughty areas, as you need to be able to control the temperature of the vivarium in order to keep your reptile healthy. Pick a room in which the temperature is fairly stable. Avoid porches, garages and other areas where the temperature is likely to fluctuate wildly.

As important as the cage itself is its covering. Snakes are active and agile and can squeeze through amazingly small spaces. It is essential that the cage has a tight-fitting lid. When I say 'tight-fitting', I mean it! Not only can snakes escape through small holes but they can push off a loose cage lid and escape. Use clips, locks or other devices to secure the lid.

The cage lid should be well ventilated with metal mesh screening. Don't use very fine mesh as some snakes rub their snouts raw on it. For all but the smallest species, 0.75cm (0.25in) mesh is ideal.

Next, the cage needs some sort of floor covering which should be disposable or easily cleaned. The snake will soil its substrate so you need to be able to remove faecal material easily and quickly, to discourage bacteria and fungi and to keep the cage smelling clean.

The cheapest, cleanest and easiest-to-remove substrate is newspaper. Unfortunately, it is not very attractive. Many snake keepers opt for astroturf or other types of indoor/outdoor plastic carpeting. Cut to size to cover the bottom of the cage, it is easily removed, rinsed, dried and replaced. There are also a number of special materials available from your pet shop.

Some keepers use sand for their snakes but this is really suitable only for desert species. The best all-round substrate is wood shavings. Not only are they absorbent, but they are cheap, easy to obtain, clean and can look good in any vivarium. Another alternative is bark chippings. These look very natural and are relatively cheap if you have only one or two vivariums.

The only substrate *not* recommended is gravel, which is not at all absorbent and is difficult to get completely clean.

Whenever you change the substrate material, wash out the cage as well. Regular disinfection helps prevent disease. Your pet shop will stock a variety of disinfectants for use with reptiles. Always make sure the vivarium is completely dry before putting your snake back. Place your snake in a sack or cotton bag for safety while you are cleaning.

Simple decoration makes cleaning easier. A large flat rock makes an excellent basking spot and some wood branches allow the snake to climb. If you use rocks and branches from outdoors, scrub them vigorously, soaking them in scalding hot water and drying them completely before use. After going to such trouble to select a parasite-free snake you don't want to introduce mites or other parasites by accident.

For the time being, do not put plants in the snake's vivarium. You have enough to learn about taking care of the snake without having to worry about keeping plants alive as well. As with other items put into the cage, the soil around the plant roots may introduce parasites. Also, although snakes don't have feet, they still crawl over plants and crush them. If you must have some greenery, why not go for one of the many plastic plants available. They are cheap, stay green and can be washed under the tap.

Like most other animals, a snake needs a secure refuge - a place to call home. The best way to provide this is to give the snake a 'hide box', an artificial cave into which it can crawl when it needs privacy. The easiest hide box is an inverted cardboard box, about the size and shape of a shoebox, with a small 'mousehole' opening cut into one end. Pet shops may stock attractive (and more durable) ceramic or plastic boxes designed specifically for the purpose. Alternatively, you can use your imagination and glue pieces of bark or rocks together with a non-toxic adhesive such as silicone cement.

Whatever the design, a hide box is an absolute necessity; snakes deprived of such shelter become stressed, may stop feeding and often succumb to disease.

Always provide water for your snake, but different species have different requirements. Some species need to soak their whole body, whilst others may never be seen near the water. Humidity is vitally important in the vivarium. If the humidity is too high your snake can develop skin blisters, breathing problems and bacterial infections. Always use clean, warm water and replace it daily, putting it in a heavy bowl your snake will not be able to tip over.

Above: Water is essential for all snakes and some species, like the Sinaloan milk snake, submerge their bodies in water.

Left: A vivarium set up ready for its occupant.

LIGHT AND HEAT

Snakes are reptiles, of course, and as such they are 'cold-blooded', an unfortunate term since the blood of an active snake may be as warm or warmer than our own. Reptiles are *behavioural thermoregulators* which means that they shuttle backwards and forwards between warm and cool spots to maintain a fairly constant internal temperature.

Use this knowledge when planning the lighting and heating of your snake vivarium by setting up a *thermal gradient*. What this means, simply, is that one end of the cage is warm, the opposite end is cool, and the distance between them has a temperature somewhere in between.

Place your heat source, either a 60-75w light bulb or a ceramic heater, at one end of the cage. This can be outside the cage above the mesh or inside, protected by mesh screening to prevent the snake burning itself. Place a large flat rock directly below as a basking surface.

You can also use a heat mat underneath the rock, which should cover about half the length of the vivarium. A heat mat is sufficient for some of the smaller species of snake but, in most cases, you will need to use a bulb or ceramic heater as well.

It is a good idea to have the main heat source on a thermostat set for about 30°C (86°F). This will ensure your snake doesn't overheat. If you have the main heat source on a timer you can also provide a cooler night-time temperature. This will be necessary if you ever go in for breeding your snake.

At the other end of the cage, place the hide box well away from the incandescent bulb. Using a thermometer, check that the temperature over the basking rock is about 24-30° (75-86°F), and that the inside of the hide box is about 10-15° cooler. Now your snake can regulate its temperature easily by moving to and fro between the rock and the hide box.

You may want to light your vivarium. Most snakes do not require lighting but you can see your snake better with a light. The species that do require lighting are garters, rough green snakes and water snakes. They need light to synthesise vitamin D and, if you choose to keep these species, you must be prepared to have a full spectrum fluorescent light on for at least ten hours a day. Even though they do not need light, many species will sit and bask under it and, of course, your vivarium will look much better when lit. Do protect the light from the snakes which have been known to burn themselves by climbing around the fittings.

FEEDING

Snakes do not use food energy to warm their bodies, so a snake needs less food than a mammal of the same size. However, as a snake's blood is far from cold and it does take food to maintain activity, do not underestimate the amount of food your snake needs.

How often a snake is fed depends on two factors. The first is the snake's size, and the second is the type of prey taken. These factors are interrelated to some degree, as we shall see.

The Eastern hognose, *Hetodon platirhinos*, is less easy to feed than its western relation.

Many species, like this Northern water snake, enjoy fish.

A small snake is usually more active than a large snake and tends to take small meals more frequently. A large snake takes larger prey less often. Small prey, such as an earthworm or goldfish, is digested fairly quickly, whereas large food, such as a rodent, takes considerably longer. To give an example, a 60cm (2ft) garter snake is satisfied with two or three meals of goldfish or earthworms per week, whereas a 1.20m (4ft) rat snake needs only one meal a week, consisting of an adult rat.

It's a little bit disgusting but here's a tip for timing feeds: keep trace of how often your snake defecates. When a snake voids waste, it has more or less completely digested its last meal and is probably hungry. In a very short time, you will know your snake's individual feeding schedule and timing feedings will be second nature.

Snakes that take larger items of food, such as rats, do not have to be fed as often as those who eat earthworms or goldfish.

For the beginners' snakes we're discussing in this book, one or more of the following foods will suffice: earthworms, fish and rodents. Earthworms are available from some pet shops and local fishing bait stores or you can find them under stones and logs in moist, loamy soil. If you collect your own, make absolutely certain that no fertilisers or pesticides have been used in the area where you catch them. Earthworms keep well in a ventilated box filled with moist leaf mould and stored in a cool, dark place such as a garage or even the refrigerator (spouses and parents just love this one!). Rinse all the soil off the worms just before feeding and give them to your snake from a shallow bowl - a plastic butter tub works well.

Garter snakes and water snakes eat fish as their main diet. Most are very good feeders and you will be amazed at how much they can eat but take care with the types of fish that you feed. Oily fish such as whitebait, sprats and lance fish contain thiaminase. This destroys vitamin B12, essential for good health. Although cooking destroys thiaminase, it is not natural for snakes to eat cooked food, so use vitamin supplements and other foods as part of the diet instead. Try scenting pinkies and earthworms with fish to encourage your snake to eat them. Strips of fish can be used in an emergency but, again, you must add vitamin supplements.

This African egg-eating snake has just swallowed a quail egg.

Most snakes eat rodents, either mice or rats, which can be bought frozen from your local reptile shop. All captive-bred snakes should be happy to feed on defrosted food. Some wild-caught snakes will need to be fed on freshly killed food and be 'weaned' on to frozen. This is best left to an experienced reptile keeper so do not buy any wild-caught snakes. Make sure that the food is thoroughly defrosted and warm to the touch. With some snakes you may need to wiggle the food in front of their faces before they will strike. Use a pair of forceps to hold the rodent's tail, which should prevent the snake from biting you by mistake.

Choose food items with care. All food should be of good quality and never more than 1.5 times the size of your snake's head. A portion of food which is too large can cause problems for your snake, which will grow just as quickly on two smaller items as on one huge one. Remember that a 'pinkie' (a baby mouse or rat without fur) is fed to hatchling snakes. 'Fuzzies' are mice or rats with a covering of fur, then there are small, medium or large rats or mice. As your snake grows, move up through the rodent sizes accordingly.

The Bull snake, *Pituophis sayi*, can grow up to 2.4m in length.

You should not need to give a vitamin supplement when using good quality food but, if you feel your snake needs a boost, use one of the special reptile vitamins available from your local pet shop. Vitamins can be placed in the rodent's mouth before feeding the snake.

Do remember that some snakes have natural fasting periods and can go up to several months without eating. Do not worry if your snake misses one or two feeds but, if it loses condition or appears to lose weight, then you must seek expert advice.

Let me finish this section by talking about the feeding of live food. When some people feed snakes occasionally they are tempted to show off to their friends by giving a live mouse or rat to the big, dangerous snake. Not only is this unlawful but it may harm your snake. Many snakes have been killed by rodents; there is no point in risking the life of your pet just to show off.

An albino variety of Boa constrictor.

DISEASES

Most diseases and parasites are difficult for the amateur to diagnose. It is better to approach the issue from the angle of prevention: select a healthy snake and keep it healthy with good diet and hygienic cage conditions.

However, we will consider just a couple of common problems. The first is external parasites, namely mites and ticks. If you have to deal with them, cut a 2.5cm (1in) square piece of Vapona fly killer (or other impregnated insecticide strip) and hang it in the cage inside a perforated plastic box or anything else that lets the insecticide out but prevents the snake from coming into direct contact with it. All the mites or ticks will be dead within days and the insecticide can be removed. An alternative is to use a pyrethrin-based spray specially made for reptiles. Do not use those designed for cats and dogs as the concentration may be too strong and kill your snake. Do not spray around the eyes, mouth or nasal passages. Internal parasites or worms are more difficult to detect and treat. If you suspect your snake is suffering from internal parasites (if it is eating well but losing weight) you must consult a veterinary surgeon.

Another common problem is shedding difficulties. A snake's skin does not grow with it and is shed roughly every six weeks. Before shedding the snake looks dull and milky, its eyes cloud over and it will refuse food. Rough-surfaced rocks or branches in the cage help the snake start to shed.

Most snakes shed without any problem but sometimes the old skin comes away in pieces. If any skin is left on the snake or it retains the eye caps, it does help to place the snake in a damp snake sack. If the eye caps still do not come off ask the help of an expert reptile keeper who will remove them with tweezers. Do not try this without being shown how.

Humidity is very important to snakes. If the vivarium is too damp it can cause skin blisters and, combined with too low a temperature, result in pneumonia. The first thing you must do is raise the temperature and lower the humidity. If no improvement is shown within 24 hours go to your veterinary surgeon.

The other problem you may come across is mouth rot. This can be identified by a cottage cheese-like substance in the mouth accompanied by a foul smell. Consult a vet immediately.

Choose your vet carefully before you need his or her services as not all are interested in treating reptiles.

THE SNAKES

Now we've got to the point of the book - the snakes themselves! What follows is a selection of the best pet snakes for beginner fanciers. I've used four criteria in deciding which snakes to include in this section: hardiness, availability, temperament and price. I've tried to pick snakes that feed well, are resistant to disease and are often seen for sale in pet shops (with the odd exception). They are also species that tame readily. Most of the snakes seen here are generally available for £100 or less - sometimes much less. Keep in mind, though, that prices vary tremendously from place to place.

First, I cannot emphasise enough - do not consider, even for a moment, purchasing a venomous snake. Some mildly venomous species are seen in pet shops and a good many more, including some truly deadly snakes, are available from breeders. These are only for the experts - people who have the experience to handle the snakes, and have the serum available in case they are bitten. Accidents do happen but do make sure you're not a victim.

The opinions presented on the following snakes are my own, based on my own experiences with them. Other authors may recommend certain species that I do not but I think almost any snake keeper will agree on the virtues of the ones I have mentioned. So, without further digression, on to our first group of snakes.

Kingsnakes

Kingsnakes have not always been regarded as the best beginners' snakes because of difficulties with wild-caught specimens but now you should never even see a wild-caught specimen for sale, let alone need to purchase one. Kingsnakes breed very well in captivity and the price of hatchlings is very reasonable. With some snakes it is not always easy to get past the hatchling stage but Kingsnakes are very willing feeders at any size and I have never seen a poor Kingsnake hatchling. Some people have been put off by the eagerness of these snakes to feed because they look as though they are constantly striking. Follow the guidelines for handling and touch their heads with a snake stick or glove before putting your hands in. It will only be a matter of weeks before you have a very gentle and tractable pet.

All the species of Kingsnake available are capable of reaching 1.80cm (6ft) in length although most only grow to 90cm-120cm (3-4ft) in captivity. The species you will see the most of is the Common kingsnake (*Lampropeltis getula*). It has many sub-species, all of which come in many colour morphs. Undoubtedly the most popular is the Californian kingsnake (*L g californiae*). The wild colour is black or dark brown with either yellow bands around the body or a yellow stripe down the back. The colour morphs, especially the albino, are now easier to obtain due to captive breeding efforts. Some of the more popular sub-species available are the Florida kingsnake (*L g floridana*), a speckled black and white snake; the heavily-marked Speckled kingsnake (*L g holbrooki*); and the Eastern kingsnake (*L g getula*) which has a yellow chain pattern on black scales. The only disadvantage with Kingsnakes is that they must be kept on their own as they eat other snakes.

Corn Snakes

The snakes most people think of when talking about beginners' snakes are corn snakes, and rightly so. Corn snakes are part of the rat snake family (genus *Elaphe*), and are very hardy and easy to keep. Sometimes called Red rat snakes because of their bright red wild colour, they have been bred in every colour morph possible and pattern morphs are now appearing.

Several sub-species are available, the most common of which is the Great Plains rat snake (*Elaphe guttata emoryi*).

Avoid any wild-caught specimens as they are often full of internal parasites. In any case, Corns breed so well in captivity that hatchlings are available everywhere. When buying Corns, try and wait until after the main breeding season. Unfortunately, because of the high demand for Corns, some breeders sell them before the hatchlings are feeding properly. This often results in disappointment for the first-time snake owner as a percentage of hatchling Corns die or are difficult to get feeding unless you have lots of experience. If you can wait that long, try to buy young Corns during the winter after they have had a chance to grow and have good feeding records.

As you may have guessed, corns eat rats, although in captivity they rarely get big enough to eat adult rats and are better on mice. In the wild they would also eat bats, birds and lizards. Corns feed by constriction, which means that they coil around their prey so tightly that the animal cannot breathe. You can feed defrosted

An albino striped Californian kingsnake.

A heavy earthenware bowl containing a little water makes a cool retreat on a hot day.

mice, but you may have to wiggle the food. Corns can grow up to 1.8m (6ft) but are more likely to reach 1.2m-1.5m (4-5ft) in captivity. Corns are great escape artists so a secure vivarium is an absolute necessity.

Gopher, Bull And Pine Snakes

The massive snakes of the genus *Pituophis* also make good pets. They look rather like rat snakes but have an almost beaked appearance due to a heavy rostral scale and somewhat recessed lower jaw; these adaptations help them in burrowing. Most are variegated in shades of black, brown and white. The scales are strongly keeled, the anal plate is single, and these snakes are much heavier than either kingsnakes or rat snakes. They are egglayers and, like kingsnakes and rat snakes, kill by constriction. All are capable of exceeding 2.4m (8ft) in length although most only reach 1.8m (6ft) in captivity.

Wild specimens do not usually bite but they hiss loudly and squirm a lot. With gentle handling they will tame easily and stop hissing. They feed on larger rodents.

In the hobby we usually see the Gopher snake (*Pituophis catenifer*), the Bull snake (*P c sayi*) and the Pine snake (*P melanoleucus*). Popular forms include an albino form of the Gopher snake plus the Black pine snake (*P m lodingi*), a melanistic subspecies of the Pine snake.

Rat Snakes

Apart from Corns, the rest of the Rat snake family can be a bit more difficult to keep. There are many different species available but many are hard to find as captive breeds. The two most common species are the Black rat snake (*Elaphe obsoleta obsoleta*), which is a stunning black, glossy snake (although albino forms are available), and the Yellow rat snake (*Elaphe obsoleta quadravittata*). This is a dark yellow snake with four brownish stripes. Yellow rats are very attractive and fairly easy to keep but can be quite aggressive.

Also available is the Everglades rat snake (*E o rossalleni*), which has the same brownish stripes as the yellow rat but with bright orange background scales. Unfortunately Everglades rats are often paired with Yellow rats to produce hybrid youngsters. These are viable snakes (in other words, they can reproduce themselves) but, if possible, look out for true Everglades with red tongues. The care of these snakes is the same as for Corn snakes.

Garter, Ribbon And Water Snakes

The Garter and Ribbon snakes, genus *Thamnophis*, are among the most familiar of North American snakes. The most common species in the hobby are the Common garter snake (*Thamnophis sirtalis*), and the Eastern ribbon snake (*T sauritus*). Other species may appear but care is similar. All species are livebearing, giving birth to about two dozen young at a time. The scales are heavily keeled and the anal plate single. These species are often aquatic, especially the ribbon snakes.

The Common garter snake appears in a baffling array of subspecies and colour

A Yellow rat snake. Rat snakes are very attractive but can be aggressive.

varieties but most are olive to blackish in colour, with three yellow longitudinal stripes. There may be plenty of yellow and red speckling. One of the attractive forms seen in pet shops is the Red-sided garter snake (*T sirtalis parietalis*). Another attractive form is a melanistic (black) variety that has no stripes. Some dedicated breeders are now cultivating this unusual form. *T sirtalis* reaches an adult length of about 90cm (3ft) in captivity, though wild specimens may reach 120cm (4ft).

As said earlier, the Eastern ribbon snake is commonly available. Occasionally, the Western ribbon snake (*T proximus*) also appears. Ribbon snakes look like (actually, are) elongated garter snakes. Ribbon snakes are usually solid black in colour, with no speckling, and brightly contrasting stripes (yellow in *T sauritus* and blue in *T proximus*). It is not uncommon for adult ribbon snakes to reach 120cm (4ft). They are highly aquatic but, in captivity, both Ribbon and Garter snakes must be kept in a dry cage. When the cage is damp, these snakes are very prone to bacterial and fungal skin infections, especially disfiguring boils, which are extremely difficult to treat.

Otherwise, both Garter snakes and Ribbon snakes are very inexpensive and very hardy. Ribbons are a little more active and nervous but usually settle down well. Both species feed on insects, worms, fish and frogs. Some may take crickets but earthworms and whole fish are better foods. Garters usually take any of these but, because of their aquatic nature, ribbon snakes may refuse anything but fish.

On the negative side, most Garter and Ribbon snakes are not captive-bred and these snakes require patient handling to tame them. They may bite vigorously at first and nearly always exude a nasty-smelling musk from their anal glands. Fortunately, both of these disagreeable habits die down in time, and Garter and Ribbon snakes become calm pets.

Water snakes are very similar to Garter snakes, only bigger. There are many species available, although most of them are a dull green or brown colour. Water snakes are much bigger than Garter or Ribbon snakes so, if they decide to exude musk over you (as they often do), the experience can be quite nasty and very smelly! The most commonly seen species is the Brown water snake (*Nerodia taxispilota*) which is usually wild caught.

All the Garters, Ribbons and Water snakes are cheap to buy but all of them require UV lighting and whole fish to remain healthy. This makes them more expensive to set up. Unfortunately, many do not survive long in captivity, as their owners become reluctant to spend money on equipment for such cheap animals.

Boas

On the whole, Boas tend to be very large snakes. I would not recommend starting with boas but have included them as many beginners are attracted by them. When these snakes are mentioned, the Common boa (*Boa constrictor*) is the first snake most people think of. The boa has gained an undeserved reputation for being a man-eating villain, growing to huge proportions and crushing to death all that comes its way.

This is all very unfair to the boas. They do not kill their prey by crushing but by constricting in the same way as a Corn snake does. As to their size, the Common boa will rarely reach its full size of 3m (10ft) in captivity and a snake of 3m or less is certainly not capable of eating a man.

A San Francisco garter snake, *Thamnophis sirtalis tetrataenia*.

The family of **Boidae** contains many different species of snake, from the very small Rubber boa which can withstand very cold temperatures to the Giant anaconda which can reach about 9m (30ft) in length. Anacondas can be very temperamental as well as big and really should not be considered suitable to have in the home.

Rosy boas, Sand boas and Rainbow boas are all small snakes at about 60cm-180cm (2ft-6ft) and should be considered as a second snake, or possibly a first snake for a responsible adult.

The Common boa has a pleasant temperament but needs considerable investment to house. A vivarium 2m x 2m x 1m (6ft x 6ft x 3ft) is the smallest I would recommend for an adult boa.

Boas are ovoviviparous, giving birth to live young, and are not as easy to breed as other snakes discussed in this book. This makes the initial purchase price of the snakes more expensive, even for the babies.

Hognose Snakes

The genus *Heterodon* contains three species, but here we discuss only the Western hognose snake (*H nasicus*), which adapts more readily to a non-amphibian diet than the other two species (*H platirhinos*, the Eastern hognose, and *H simus*, the Southern hognose). These are heavy-bodied snakes with dark brown blotching on grey. The scales are heavily keeled and the anal plate is divided. *H nasicus* reaches about 90cm (3ft) in length, making it a medium size snake in this group.

A Hognose snake has a curious hooked snout, which it uses like a garden spade to burrow after its favourite prey, toads. It is quite easy to persuade the Western hognose to take pinkie mice as an alternative to toads, although you may need to use a bit of deception at first. The trick is to take a pinkie and simply rub the rodent

well with a dead toad. It really works! After a while, the snake takes the pinkies without any problem.

A substrate of dry shredded bark provides the best burrowing medium in captivity for these snakes.

Hognoses are among the most fascinating of all snakes because of their unusual defensive behaviour. When threatened, a Hognose hisses loudly, flattens its head and neck and strikes with open mouth, yet it stops short of biting. If the disturbance continues, it suddenly convulses and rolls over on its back, apparently dead. When the tormentor departs, the snake soon rights itself and crawls away. After a while, it will lose this tendency to bluff and play dead. In fact, a captive-bred specimen will probably already be tame as these snakes become docile very rapidly.

Pythons

Many people might argue that Pythons should come higher in this list of recommendations but most of these snakes cause some sort of difficulty for the prospective owner. The two species most commonly available are the Burmese python (*Python molurus bivittatus*) which can reach 6m (20ft) or more, and the small, gentle Royal python (*Python regius*), which can be the most difficult of feeders.

Avoid both of these species until you have some experience with reptiles. Burmese pythons grow large very quickly and can be difficult to feed as hatchlings, even when captive-bred. Some have been known to get temperamental and a 6m snake with behavioural problems is not much fun!

Royal pythons are usually wild-caught, although most hatchlings are captive farmed. This is where eggs are removed from wild females and incubated in large pits in the ground. Although hatchlings feed better than wild-caught adults, there are all too many stories of them starving to death before their inexperienced owners learn how to feed these beautiful but fussy snakes.

An Indian python. Pythons are not recommended for novice snake-keepers.

The Corn snake, *Elaphe guttata guttata*, is the ideal beginner's snake.

ODDS AND ENDS

This section touches briefly on a couple of important topics, which I have grouped together for convenience.

I would be negligent if I did not mention the issues of collection and conservation. With many snake species on the decline in their natural habitats, collecting wild snakes is to be discouraged. Wherever possible, only buy captive-bred snakes. Apart from not having to remove a wild snake from its habitat, there are more practical reasons for selecting captive-bred snakes over wild-caught: the former are invariably healthier, more dependable eaters and more docile as pets.

I would also like to urge you to join a local herpetology club. There are more of these than you might think; there is almost certainly a regional club near you or you could join a national society. A pet shop or library should be able to tell you if there is such a group in your area. If there isn't, you may wish to start one. Such clubs are invaluable sources of information and will help the beginner evolve into an expert. Don't underestimate the social value - it's good to meet people with a common interest.

This red-tailed racer has just sloughed its skin.

LOOKING AHEAD

In time, you'll find that you will no longer be satisfied with just one snake and you'll be ready to move on to more challenging species. Here are just a few to whet your appetite.

Milk snakes, or tricolour kings, are black, red, and yellow (or white) banded forms of *Lampropeltis triangulum* and a few other species. These are gorgeous snakes but they can be fussy feeders - most eat lizards and snakes and, although they will adapt to a rodent diet, often it takes patience on the part of the keeper. These are good intermediate-level snakes for the hobbyist who already has experience with easier species.

There are also many more Rat snakes than the ones considered in this book, including some colourful Asian species. However, many of these are more temperamental than their North American counterparts.

You may also wish to try Racers and Whipsnakes (*Coluber* and *Masticophis* respectively). These are slender, high-strung and aggressive, but also beautiful. There are also some odd Boas and Pythons, such as the arboreal Emerald tree boa (*Corallus caninus*) and Green tree python (*Chondropython viridus*).

A Yellow anaconda.

An albino Milk snake.

The possibilities go on and on. Eventually you may wish to breed your snakes, something that hobbyists are accomplishing more frequently these days. This requires you to pay even more attention to detail than with your first snake, especially with regard to nutrition and lighting, both of which are critical factors for getting snakes 'in the mood'. You will also have to learn how to hibernate most species if you intend to breed them.

And, some day, even snakes may not be enough ...... you'll move on to lizards, terrapins and amphibians. As the saying goes, a little knowledge is a dangerous thing! The quest for herpetological information can become quite a passion.

But that's in the future. These and other species can be long-term goals but, for now, concentrate on and enjoy your first snake.

BIBLIOGRAPHY

The Completely Illustrated Atlas of Reptiles and Amphibians for the Terrarium
Fritz Jurgen Obst, Dr Klaus Richter and Dr Udo Jacob
ISBN 0-86622-958-2
H-1102

This volume is the perfect answer to the terrarium keeper's dilemma of attempting to find where an animal originated and what type of habitat it requires. It is the obvious first place to look for a solution or a hint to all your questions while having fun looking at the marvellous photos at the same time.

Pythons and Boas
Peter J Stafford
ISBN 0-86622-084-4
PS-846

Here's the first authoritative work on the Boas and Pythons, an attractive - and very colourful - volume that answers every question about snake care and presents current information on Boas and Pythons in a comprehensive book.

The Mini-Atlas of Snakes of the World
John Coborn
ISBN: 0-86622-601-X
TS-193

This invaluable work is a comprehensive guide to snakes, being a quick and reliable reference to identification, food preferences, mode of reproduction, potential harmfulness and average adult length.

Useful Address

The British Herpetological Society
c/o Zoological Society of London
Regents Park
London NW1 4RY
Tel: 020 8452 9578